The Essential Buyer's Guide

LOTUS
SEVEN REPLICAS & CATERHAM 7

1973 to 2013

Your marque expert:
Rob Hawkins

VELOCE PUBLISHING
THE PUBLISHER OF FINE AUTOMOTIVE BOOKS

The Essential Buyer's Guide Series

www.veloce.co.uk

First published in June 2013, reprinted August 2020 by Veloce Publishing Limited, Veloce House, Parkway Farm Business Park, Middle Farm Way, Poundbury, Dorchester, Dorset, DT1 3AR, England.
Tel 01305 260068/Fax 01305 250479/e-mail info@veloce.co.uk/web www.veloce.co.uk or www.velocebooks.com.

ISBN: 978-1-845844-86-8 UPC: 6-36847-04486-2

Introduction
– the purpose of this book

The Lotus Seven has become a worldwide inspiration for a wide range of similarly styled cars – which form the basis of this book.

The marque was launched in 1957, after which time it underwent several revisions (Series 1-4) before Caterham Cars took it on in 1973 and has manufactured it ever since. Copies, recreations, and variations of the Seven have created just as much attention and popularity as the original Lotus, or the Caterham 7. Westfield, Dax, Sylva, Tiger, GBS and MK are just some of the manufacturers that have created kits and cars with similar styling – often with their own approach to performance and handling: few have attempted to recreate the original Lotus Seven exactly.

Seven replicas are supported by a wide variety of clubs, forums and motoring groups, and are often seen at car shows.

The true successor to the Lotus Seven is made by Caterham Cars, which acquired the rights in 1973.

Many recreations of the original are only associated with the Lotus Seven because of the unique styling of such cars, but this is as vague as classifying all estate cars as the same. Consequently, the purpose of this book is to arm the reader with the knowledge required to carefully consider all options before buying what is classed as a Lotus Seven replica. After reading this book, you will be familiar with the various engine options which have been tried and tested over the years, the different suspension and brake setups, body styling, and chassis designs.

3

Driving a Seven replica is an essential requirement for a true car enthusiast. You won't be disappointed by the raw performance.

The Lotus Seven replica market has opened up over the last 10-15 years to accommodate a wide range of budgets. There are home-build kits that range from a book instructing how to make your own chassis, right up to turnkey cars, which have never been available as a DIY package.

If you're a car enthusiast, a Lotus Seven replica has got to be on your list of vehicles to own. It presents seat-of-your-pants motoring with minimal creature comforts. Don't expect a car that can be used as a practical everyday run around, but do prepare yourself for an education in sports car motoring where performance and handling can teach you everything a modern car cannot.

No matter what your budget, there's a car or abandoned project to suit your funds, and whether you're a novice mechanic or trained engineer, these cars are simple to maintain and straightforward to work on.

There's a worldwide community of Seven replica owners that are associated with dedicated or general clubs, forums, or the occasional show. Most are only too willing to help, and accept whichever model you may want to own, based purely on a common interest. So, if you're keen to join in, read on!

Books showing how to make just about every part for a Lotus Seven replica have helped to widen the appeal of these cars.

Contents

The Essential Buyer's Guide™ currency
At the time of publication a BG unit of currency "●" equals approximately
£1.00/US$1.32/Euro 1.11. Please adjust to suit current exchange rates
using Sterling as the base currency.

1 Is it the right car for you?
– marriage guidance

A Lotus Seven replica is a true enthusiast's car that will appeal to anyone who wants a taste of raw sports car performance. Depending on how well the car has been built, its level of refinement can be positively luxurious, or increasingly frustrating – especially if your legs get cooked from the heat of the engine, your face gets battered by the wind, and your fillings start to loosen over every lump in the road.

It's fair to say that a Lotus Seven replica isn't an everyday car, although many owners would disagree as they can be made to be practical. They have the potential for long-distance motoring, with various means of accommodating luggage.

Can a car such as this Caterham 7 be treated in a similar manner to a modern production car?

This chapter explores all the practical considerations of owning a Lotus Seven replica, from size and driving characteristics, to running costs and spares.

Tall and short drivers

One of the biggest problems of the Lotus Seven replica market concerns interior space and accommodation for taller drivers, but there are several solutions available. Many manufacturers, including Caterham, Westfield, Tiger, and Great British Sports Cars, have created cars with wider and longer cockpits to ensure drivers who exceed 6.5ft can fit in them. It's also feasible to fit seats on runners, so both tall and short drivers can operate such a car. Seating, however, is only one issue. Pedal space is another potential problem, and it's essential to make sure you can operate all three pedals

Make sure you can get in and out of the driving seat and operate the pedals.

without catching two of them at a time. You may want to invest in a narrow pair of racing shoes, but if you have wide feet, and the pedals in a particular car are close together, you may have to walk away if you can't operate it safely.

Headroom can be another issue, especially if a windscreen and hood are fitted. In such cases, ask for the hood to be erected, and make sure you can sit inside with sufficient room between the top of your head and the roof or framework.

Driving

Lotus Seven replicas represent traditional rear-wheel drive motoring, but a poorly set up or built car could put you off. The wrong suspension spring rates – with stiff dampers and heavy unsprung weight (wheels, hubs, uprights, brakes) – can result in a bone-jarring ride quality that becomes annoying instead of addictive. The steering should be light, the brakes responsive (despite usually being non-servo assisted), and the engine lively for such a light car. However, there's more to how these cars will drive: it all depends on what components have been fitted, and whether they have been set up correctly.

Live axle or IRS

There are two main differences at the rear of most Lotus Seven replicas. Early examples used a live axle from cars, including the Ford Escort Mk2. Such a setup can use panhard rods, vertical coilovers, and fore-and-aft arms to keep the axle in position. The majority of cars now feature an independent rear suspension setup, with a Ford Sierra differential mounted in the chassis,

A live axle setup often feels harsher on the road than an IRS.

and the hubs and uprights secured with upper and lower double wishbones (other rear suspension setups are mentioned later in this book). The latter is often more compliant on the road, but many people prefer a live axle for racing.

Bike or car

There are two differences when it comes to engines found in Lotus Seven replicas: motorbike, or car power, and each has its own list of considerations. Motorbike power is exhilarating, especially with a paddle shift operating a sequential gearbox, which results in fast gear changes at 10,000+rpm. However, it may be all noise and no-go if the car isn't light enough (450-500kg max), and motorbike gearboxes have no reverse, so check whether an aftermarket electric conversion or similar has been fitted if you intend to drive backwards.

The Ford Zetec engine is usually found in the Mondeo and Focus, but makes for a practical and reliable motor in a Lotus Seven replica.

Car engines generally range from the Ford OHV, crossflow, and SOHC Pinto, to a wide range of twin cams (Ford Zetec, Toyota 4AGE, K-series) and V8s. Performance can be just as exhilarating as a motorbike-engine, but with fewer revs.

Motorbike engines are neat and compact, and can add a Formula One feel to a car.

Interior space

The minimalist design of the original Lotus Seven is often transferred to replicas, and despite several manufacturers having managed to create wider and longer cockpits, these cars are never going to be as spacious internally as modern sports cars such as the MGF or Mazda MX-5. Depending on the car you are looking to buy, and how much thought has gone into the build of the interior, the choice of seats and the fitting of panels can either make the most of the space available, or occupy the majority of it.

Luggage capacity

Some Lotus Seven replicas have a small boot incorporated in to the rear, above the axle. This may not be as deep as expected, as the fuel tank is also

Great British Sports Cars has created a narrow (foreground) and wide-bodied Zero, to help accommodate larger drivers.

Determined to travel: towing a caravan is one solution to a lack of luggage and accommodation space.

Boot depth can be shallow because there's a fuel tank and axle underneath.

fitted here. Many manufacturers have developed lockable boots, however, which can accommodate a few small items of luggage. If a roll bar is fitted, it's feasible to tie luggage to it. Some owners have resorted to other means of carrying luggage, such as fitting a towbar, in order to pull a trailer or a small caravan.

Wet weather protection

Many Lotus Seven replicas are built without a full windscreen, as this is easier to complete, and for tests such as the IVA (Individual Vehicle Approval), it means

A windscreen, doors, and a hood can keep out the rain.

you don't have to fit windscreen wipers and a heater/demister. However, many manufacturers produce windscreens, doors, and hoods to provide all-weather protection. Some are fiddly to fit, and once fitted, you'll have to hope the heater is good at demisting (manufacturers including Caterham and Tiger produce a heated windscreen to demist the glass).

Will it fit in the garage?

Most garages – including those found in modern homes – can accommodate a Lotus Seven replica.

The dimensions of most Lotus Seven replicas is less than a Ford Focus. Generally, the overall length is around 3.3m (no more than 11ft). The width is usually similar to donor vehicles, including the Ford Escort Mk2 and Sierra, due to the use of the rear axle or hubs, diff, and driveshafts (around 1.7m). The height of a Lotus Seven replica shouldn't present any garage problems, unless you intend to stack them!

Running costs

Car tax in the UK can be relatively cheap on motorbike engines, which are often below the 1549cc limit, meaning the cheaper rate applies.

Fuel costs vary according to engine and fuelling. As a rough guide, a car engine such as a Ford Zetec that's fuelled by two Weber carburettors may return 25-30mpg, but can be more frugal (40mpg) with a fuel-injection system.

Tyre wear is often minimal because these cars are lightweight, and don't cover tens of thousands of miles each year (note that tyres have a recommended lifespan, even if they are not worn). Similarly, brake pads and discs don't seem to wear quickly.

Parts availability

There is a vast assortment of specialists who can supply parts for these cars, ranging from scrapyards with donor vehicles, to performance stockists including Demon Tweeks, Rally Design, and Burton Power, who have developed many specific parts for these cars. Kit car building experts, including Car Builder Solutions and Europa Spares, also sell useful parts to help keep these cars on the road. Be aware that some parts may be more expensive than expected. For instance, if performance brake pads and discs have been fitted, don't expect a new set to be a similar price to that for a Ford Mondeo, for example.

Repair costs

The DIY approach to Lotus Seven replicas means that most repairs are

Body parts are often made from GRP and are readily available, or easy to repair.

cheap: providing you are willing to think
around a problem and work it out. If
the rear body of a car is damaged, for
instance, it is probably made from GRP,
so a repair is a feasible alternative to
sourcing a new one.

Some parts are universal – such
as front cycle wings – so you can shop
around, but always check the dimensions to make sure. Many parts can be made
from raw materials, including aluminium side panels and floors.

Some repair costs can be unavoidably expensive. If you've destroyed the Suzuki
Hayabusa engine in your Lotus Seven replica, then a secondhand replacement will
cost around 2500. Some components are expensive because of their demand or
complexity, so if you want a cheap to repair Lotus Seven replica, look for one that
uses readily available donor components from a Mazda MX-5, or Ford, for instance.

Insurance

There are a number of insurance specialists who know their kit cars, and can
provide competitive, fully-comprehensive cover at a reasonable price. Unlike mass
manufactured high-performance sports cars, Lotus Seven replicas are often not
regarded on a similar level. Chapter 16 includes contact details of suitable insurers.

Investment potential

The Lotus Seven replica market covers a broad range of prices: from the home-
built Locusts, Locosts, and Haynes Roadsters, to the easy-build and turnkey
Caterhams and Westfields. Caterhams are some of the slowest depreciating models
of all sports cars;
so too are many
mid-priced Seven
replicas, such as
the Tiger R6. At
the cheap end of
the price scale,
there's investment
potential in buying
a part-built project,
finishing, and
selling it.

As a general
rule, secondhand

Lotus Seven replicas don't depreciate much, but unless you have a collectible model, they also don't appreciate without having to make improvements.

Failings
These cars are not as practical as a modern sports car, such as a Mazda MX-5, so if you intend to use one regularly, expect to limit your luggage, get wet when it rains, and never leave a car park in a hurry, as there will usually be a few people wanting to ask questions.

Plus points
Anyone who likes cars needs to own a Lotus Seven replica and experience what no-frills, rear-wheel driving, sports car performance is all about. There's so much you can learn from these cars concerning chassis design, suspension set up, handling, and performance.

Minus points
A poorly built car may be better to strip down and build again. The ride quality can be bone-jarring and disappointing if the suspension hasn't been properly set up and heavy components are used for the uprights, hubs, brakes and wheels (contributing to excessive unsprung weight). A modern Ford Ka can be quicker to drive than a Lotus Seven, that crashes over the lumps in the road and is a handful on the corners, but this is down to problems with the build, and the choice of components.

Four-seater Vindicator Family is a brave alternative to the Lotus Seven.

Alternatives
The Lotus Seven has a distinctive style that many manufacturers have followed, however kit cars, including the Sylva/Raw Striker, Dutton Phaeton, and Vindicator Sprint, are similar in their components and general design, but not in their looks. They offer an alternative to the Lotus Seven, and some people would argue that many of them are better. Of the modern equivalents of the Lotus Seven, the most promising are the exo-skeletal Aerial Atoms, KTM X-Bows, SDR V-Storms and MEV Exocets and Rockets. These cars are popular alternatives to the Seven, but could never replace it.

2 Cost considerations
– affordable, or a money pit?

Abandoned projects

Most people regard abandoned builds as the best value Lotus Seven replicas to buy, however, picking up the pieces of someone else's project can be a disaster, and may take longer than if you had bought a brand new kit. Be cautious with promises that a project is 95% complete and only requires minor wiring. If this is the case, why hasn't the owner completed the build? Similarly, if an abandoned project is being sold with all the required parts, make sure that they are definitely all there. Missing components for the brakes, electrics, and suspension can soon add up.

An abandoned project may be cheap, but make sure you won't have to undo all of the completed work.

Engine costs

Engines can be as cheap as chips, or painfully expensive, depending on the make that has been installed, and whether it has been modified. At the cheap end of the scale, engines such as the Ford Kent crossflow, Pinto, and Zetec, are some of the best motors for your money. Parts are readily available, and they are straightforward to fix. Performance purists may sniff at a dated Ford crossflow with overhead valves, but these engines are easy to work on, and offer an entertaining

Brand new Ford engines are often cheaper than a rebuild.

Motorbike engines can be expensive to rebuild. Stripping a bike and selling the unwanted parts can often be the cheapest approach.

amount of performance for the road. Others including Toyota's 4AGE twin cam from the MR2 and the Mazda 1.6/1.8 from the MX-5 are reliable and lively with around 120-130bhp at the flywheel; cheap, serviceable items, and a reputation for being bullet-proof.

Consider the cost of replacing an engine should you need to. There are three general solutions here. The first is to rebuild it yourself, which is a good idea if you want to build a highly modified motor. However, if you want a standard engine, there are, in many cases, off-the-shelf motors with guarantees, and even secondhand engines with warranties. Manufacturers including Great British Sports Cars often sell brand new crated Ford Zetec engines for around ●650 plus VAT. The cheapest solution is to buy a secondhand engine from a donor vehicle. This is often the less-painful answer for motorbike engines, where rebuild costs can be expensive, due to the high price of parts.

Brakes, suspension and steering components
Most Lotus Seven replicas use a number of common parts, especially when it comes to the brakes, suspension, and steering. The following list provides approximate prices for some popular parts:

Austin Maxi bottom ball joint (front lower wishbone) ●20
Ford Transit drag link (front upper wishbone) ●10
Ford Escort Mk2 steering rack ●120
Ford Escort Mk2 quick rack ●300
Track rod end ●10
Ford Sierra front wheel bearing ●25
Ford Sierra front brake calliper ●40
Performance brake pads for Ford Sierra from ●40

This Ford Transit drag link is a popular front suspension component for the upper wishbone.

Aftermarket parts
Specialists including Rally Design, Burton Power, Europa Spares, and Car Builder Solutions, stock a wide range of parts that are suitable for Lotus Seven replicas. Here are a few examples:

Brake master cylinder ●30
Electric radiator cooling fan ●50
Silicone hose kit ●100
Compact battery ●80
Fuel pressure regulator ●35
Wilwood rear brake calliper with handbrake ●120 each

Coilovers are manufactured by the likes of Spax, Gaz, and Protech.

Windscreen washer pump 12
Compact heater/demister 170
Coilover 75 each
Bellhousing (Ford Type 9 to Toyota 4AGE) 240

Donor parts

Cars including the Ford Sierra and Mazda MX-5 form the basis of many kit cars, including Lotus Seven replicas. It

Stripping a donor vehicle can provide a useful collection of spares.

can often be cheaper to buy a complete car, strip it down, and sell off any unwanted bits, rather than buy all the individual parts you need.

Another approach to acquiring parts is to look online at forums, classifieds such as Pistonheads, and auction sites such as eBay. Parts are often available, and bargains can be found.

Westfield parts

The following parts are listed in Westfield's starter-kit price list as optional extras, and help to illustrate what is available from many Lotus Seven replica kit car manufacturers:

Locking boot lid 375
Aero screen and Perspex 287
Rear valance 240

Kit Spares parts

Kit Spares (www.kitspares.co.uk) is part of Great British Sports Cars, which manufactures the Zero. They sell a number of universal parts that can be fitted to most Lotus Seven replicas. Here are a few examples:

Universal seat runners 23
Ford Zetec exhaust manifold 175
Fuel tank 123
Front cycle wings 96
Rear diffuser 185
Reconditioned Type 9 gearbox 594
Reconditioned Sierra diff 420

3 Living with a Seven replica
– will you get along together?

If you intend to use a Lotus Seven replica on the road, there are a few issues to consider that can at first seem irrelevant, but could result in a car being neglected in the garage, or sold on.

The first concerns ride quality: a quick test drive of a prospective purchase, whether as a passenger or driver, rarely allows you to fully assess the ride quality of a car. A well set up car with fine-tuned suspension settings, suitable springs and dampers and lightweight hubs, uprights, brakes and wheels (unsprung weight) will feel nimble and refined when driven over rough roads. Such qualities often come at a price, and are difficult to fully appreciate unless you have driven a car for more than a twenty minute test run. However, these qualities will make you want to drive the car whenever the opportunity arises, not leave it in the garage.

A bike carb kit with ignition and fuelling management is cheaper than a full-blown aftermarket fuel injection and engine management system.

If ride quality is an important factor when choosing a Lotus Seven replica, look for models that offer adjustable suspension settings, especially for camber. Adjustable spring collars on the coilovers will allow the car to be corner-

Motorbike carburettors have become a popular bridge between Webers or Dellortos and a fuel injection system.

weighted (the ride height is adjusted to balance the weight distribution between the front and rear wheels). Adjustable dampers enable you to test different settings for a firmer or softer ride.

Unsprung weight is difficult to fully assess when looking at a prospective purchase. If the uprights are lightweight, for instance, they will be made of aluminium and will be easy to identify. Similarly, lightweight brake callipers and wheels will be constructed from aluminium.

Bike engines offer extreme lightweight performance. This turbo-powered Hayabusa produces around 300bhp.

Tyres should also be considered for ride quality. A higher profile provides a softer ride over low profile tyres. Many cars use 13-15in wheels, which allow high profile tyres to be fitted.

The brakes on a Lotus Seven replica should be up to the same standard as a modern car, although they probably won't be servo-assisted, so may not feel quite as light. Some builds use the wrong internal bores for the brake master cylinder, or race pads that need to be warm to be effective, resulting in wooden brakes that can be scary. There is no excuse for poor brakes because the right components are available.

Other considerations concerning driving a Lotus Seven replica include noise. If panels have been poorly fitted, they will rattle. There's no escaping engine noise, but if a loud exhaust has been fitted, it can become annoying, overshadowing its effectiveness

Adjusting damper settings can help to alter the ride quality.

(quieter exhaust systems are available in most cases).

The heat from the engine can travel through into the footwell, especially if the panelling isn't double-skinned. This may be a bonus on a cold day, but a problem in summer when it's hot. Similarly, if you intend to drive your car during winter, you may want to buy one with a windscreen to protect your face and fingers. Even with a helmet and gloves, a car without a windscreen gets cold when driven in winter.

Consider the practicality of driving a Lotus Seven replica with particular engines. A highly tuned car engine with wild camshafts, for instance, may be sluggish below

Ride-height adjustable coilovers allow a car to be corner weighted and balanced for better handling.

Side draught Weber or Dellorto carbs are traditional, but often less fuel-efficient than an injection system.

4000rpm, and uncontrollable above. While this may seem like a challenge when first driving, it will eventually become frustrating, and is potentially dangerous. Similarly, some motorbike engines may sound fantastic, but they are much easier to stall than a car engine – especially on hill starts – and some require at least 3000rpm to get going. Plus, no gearboxes for motorbike engines have a reverse, so if you definitely want to travel backwards, make sure a reverse system is fitted (eg electric reverse), or that you can source and fit one yourself.

The type of engine and its ancillaries, including fuelling, ignition and engine management, are important considerations. In general, a carburettor fed engine is less fuel-efficient than a fuel-injected equivalent, however, fuel-injection requires

Exhaust systems can be noisy, or refined, depending largely on the quality of the silencer.

Lightweight adjustable components can help to achieve a refined ride quality that doesn't break your back.

some form of engine management to make it work, whereas carburettors don't. Some people have experimented with motorbike carburettors, which are often more fuel-efficient than traditional Weber or Dellorto side draught carburettors, and still don't require any engine management.

Many engines are now equipped with engine management to help control the ignition timing and fuelling. Specialists such as Omex, Webcon and DTA produce programmable ECUs that are popular within the kit car market, and are straightforward to install and work with. These systems can be used with modern fuel injection and ignition coil packs, helping to reduce emissions and refine performance.

To sum up what has been covered in this chapter, the beauty of most Lotus Seven replicas is that whatever aspect you may be unhappy with on a particular car, it can be changed.

There are numerous other considerations concerning interior space, spares, repairs and costs, which have been highlighted in the previous two chapters. Most of them so far have been aimed towards anyone wanting to buy a Lotus Seven replica to use on the road. There are many people that use their cars on race circuits, however: whether for dedicated competitions or occasional trackdays. Such cars often require a different set of priorities, concerning race regulation equipment for competition use (approved roll cage, seating and harness), or suitable seating and harnesses to make sure you are firmly strapped in to position when tearing round a race circuit on a trackday. In such cases, subjects such as suspension and ride quality still need to be considered. Brakes need to be able to cope with harsh application, and may need to be uprated. Lotus Seven replicas are ideal for trackdays and racing, and fortunately most manufacturers and specialists have the knowledge to help.

Refinement and ride quality are not as important on a race circuit as on the road.

4 Relative values
– which model for you?

There is a varied range of Lotus Seven replicas, so prices for complete cars can vary; ranging from ⬤2000 for a home-built but abandoned Locost, to ⬤30,000 and beyond for a top of the range Caterham 7 with a few thousand miles on the clock. The following table attempts to illustrate an approximate price structure for many of these cars, and how their values relate to other Lotus Seven replicas and recreations. Using percentage values, a top class secondhand Caterham 7 currently costs around ⬤25,000 in the UK, so the table below uses this value as 100%. A Robin Hood in similar top class condition will probably cost around ⬤5000, which is 20% of the value of ⬤25,000.

Model(s)	Top class	Good	Abandoned
Caterham 7, Donkervoort	100%	80%	40%
Westfields, Dax Rush	90%	60%	30%
MK, Tigers, MNR, Zero, Mac#1, Striker	40%	30%	20%
Locost, Locust, Haynes Roadster, Robin Hood	20%	15%	10%

There are several approaches to buying a Lotus Seven replica, largely based on how much money you are able to spend. A limited budget doesn't necessarily mean you can't have a well-known replica such as a Westfield, although it often means you may have a little more work to do.

Whilst knowing your budget is important, what's equally essential is to know your prices, and to thoroughly research current market values by studying the classifieds in kit car magazines (*Kit Car*, *Total Kit Car* and *Complete Kit Car*), online classifieds such as Pistonheads, eBay, and the many dedicated clubs and forums. You'll soon get a clear idea of how much these cars sell for, and whether you want to buy a half-finished or crash damaged project, a new kit, or an older model.

Pistonheads.com has a classifieds section for kit cars, as well as sections for Caterham and Westfield. (Courtesy Pistonheads.com)

Build or buy?
Building a Lotus Seven replica is the best approach if you want a car with a particular specification, and have the time, tools and skills to do the work yourself. Despite there being books and websites that claim you can build such a car for as little as ⬤250, most people find they spend a lot more money because they purchase performance products and don't make all of the parts themselves. Consequently, a typical build starts at around ⬤5000, in most cases.

Budget builds are not always the best approach. A complete kit for a Caterham 7 for instance, costs from

Kit cars built in the UK need to go through an Individual Vehicle Approval (IVA) before they can be registered for use on the road.

●19,995 and requires one to two weeks to build. This may sound expensive when compared with the budget builds, but all parts are brand new, and the resale values of these cars is such that depreciation is very low, so you probably won't lose much money when it comes to selling the car.

Building a Seven replica kit car is often a more financially practical approach, especially if you can spread the cost. However, always anticipate the unforeseen costs, such as registration and IVA (Individual Vehicle Approval) in the UK for amateur-built cars, that costs at least ●500.

Crash damaged

When a Lotus Seven replica is involved in a crash, front end damage often includes bent suspension wishbones, cracked cycle wings and nose cones, and punctured radiators. Such damage can often be repaired with new parts. Even if the chassis is damaged, sections can be removed and new tubing welded in place. At the rear; bodywork, suspension, and chassis damage can be similarly repaired.

If you are viewing a potential purchase that is crash damaged, check whether the parts are available from the manufacturer or a specialist. If you need to remove the rear bodywork for instance, find out whether it is bonded on to the chassis, as this will require you to cut it away.

Crash damaged projects may need an identity inspection before they can be used on the road again. In the UK, this is called the VIC (Vehicle Identity Check) and isn't a structural test of the repairs, but a check to ensure the identity of the vehicle is correct (ie the VIN plates are present).

A crash damaged car can often be a cheap approach to buying a Lotus Seven replica: providing you have the skills to complete the necessary repairs.

Budget Seven replicas

The very early Lotus Seven replicas started with models including the Locust from JC Auto Patterns of Sheffield (not to be confused with the Locost). This Triumph or Cortina-based Seven replica used wooden and aluminium body panels. The kit has moved on to new owners, and over the years was known as the Hornet and Locust ES. Whilst this was one of the early budget-styled Seven replicas, the market for these cars exploded in 2000 following the publication of Ron

Robin Hoods sold in masses, and now have a strong and active owners' club that meets at most kit car shows.

The Haynes Roadster is supported by a book showing how to make all the required parts, and uses the Ford Sierra as a donor vehicle.

Champion's book, *Build Your Own Sports Car for as little as £250*. This book showed how to make your own chassis and body panels to create your own Lotus Seven replica. Consequently, kit cars such as the Locost emerged and opened up a generic market for the Lotus Seven replica, with many specialists and manufacturers selling nose cones, chassis, suspension components, and cycle wings.

There are several other books that show how to build a Seven replica on a budget, a popular example being the Haynes Roadster. Whilst many people choose not to build everything from scratch, this alternative approach has resulted in many budget Seven replicas.

There are also many Seven-styled replicas that appeal to the cheap end of the market, one of the most popular being from Robin Hood – which created its first replica in 1988 – featuring a spaceframe chassis and using Triumph TR7 donor components. Over the years, a variety of designs and donor vehicles have been used, ranging from the Triumph Dolomite to the Ford Sierra. Robin Hood produced the Exmo, 3A and 2B, which all follow the styling of the Lotus Seven. It adopted a different approach to its kits with a monocoque shell, instead of a separate chassis. During 1996 and 1997 sales of Robin Hoods peaked at over 500 kits per year.

Budget Seven replicas generally cost around ⬤2000 upwards – depending on condition and specification – with some models being more desirable than others. Robin Hoods, for instance, appear to attract a higher price, possibly due to their popularity and recognition.

The Zero from Great British Sports Cars is a Ford or Mazda MX-5-based kit.

Tiger, Westfield, MK, GBS
If you have between ⬤5000 and ⬤10,000 to spend, then there are a lot of Seven replicas to choose from. Early Westfields with a live axle at the rear appear to start at around ⬤5000, whereas later models are often at the top end of this price bracket. Some models from the budget category can sell for over ⬤5000, if they are an outstanding build or a high specification. The majority of Seven replicas in this price bracket include the Avon and R6 from Tiger, the MK Indy, the Zero from Great British Sports Cars, MNR's VortX, the Mac#1, and the Ford Pinto-engined Dax Rush, which was also powered by a Rover V8 and usually sells for ⬤15,000 or more.

This 2004 K-series-powered Caterham 7 R400 sold for around ⬤32,000 when it was brand new, and hasn't depreciated much. Typical secondhand prices now range from ⬤22,000 to ⬤25,000.

Caterham, Donkervoort
At the high end of Lotus Seven replica pricing, there are numerous examples to be found. A brand new turnkey Seven replica manufactured by Great British

Sports Cars, Tiger Racing, and most of the other manufacturers mentioned, will cost between ●15,000 and ●20,000. Within this price bracket you will also find secondhand, high-specification, or recently registered Caterham 7s and similar models, including the Donkervoort from the Netherlands. Secondhand prices in some cases are not much cheaper than brand new, especially for Caterham 7s, where depreciation is very slow.

Dutton Phaetons were the kit car to build in the Eighties. Nowadays there's an active owners' club, and these cars are becoming collectible.

There are a number of Westfields that hold their value, including the Rover V8 engined Seight, the Suzuki Hayabusa engined Megabusa, and Honda Fireblade powered Megablade.

Sevenish styled

If you are not looking for a true recreation of a Lotus Seven, then there are numerous kit cars that are styled along the lines of the Lotus Seven, but do not attempt to recreate it. Many of the aforementioned cars fall into this category, but others, ranging from the Dutton Phaeton to the Vindicator Sprint and Raw Striker, do not bear any resemblance to the Lotus Seven, other than the use of cycle wings in some cases, and a rear wheel drive layout with a long bonnet. Many of these kit cars are popular alternatives. Dutton's Phaeton and the 2+2 Melos sold in their thousands throughout the Eighties, offering the chance to build a kit car on a tight budget. Nowadays, such cars are becoming collectible, and prices appear to start at around ●1500. Possibly the most successful kit car, which had its own distinctive styling that helped to tell it apart from a Lotus Seven, was the Sylva Striker: now known as the Raw Striker. This first appeared in 1985, and has had a successful career within racing. Just about every popular engine has been fitted to these cars, ranging from motorbike to Ford (crossflow, Pinto, Zetec, Duratec), K-series, Toyota twin-cams, and Rover V8s. Early Strikers with a live axle at the rear can be bought for upwards of ●3000, whereas later models with IRS and a modern engine cost around ●8000, or more.

The Striker is one of the most successful alternatives to the Seven. The early model on the right has evolved into the one on the left, which looks more like a modern Seven replica.

Modern Sevens

Many designers and manufacturers have attempted to create a modern version of the Lotus Seven, including Tiger's Aviator, the CC Cyclone, the Mirach, and the MEV Sonic. Many of these cars use similar components to the Lotus Seven replicas, although some are mid-engined.

Tiger Aviator was designed by Simon Keys, and is a modern interpretation of the Lotus Seven.

5 Before you view
– be well informed

Pre-checks
Before viewing a potential purchase Seven replica, there are a number of checks you can make. First, ask for the registration number and conduct an HPI check. This will establish if there is any remaining finance on the car, whether it has been stolen, crash damaged, or even written-off. There are a number of different vehicle history checking companies like HPI; all incur a fee, and offer a range of information.

Some checks are free. In the UK, for instance, visit motinfo.direct.gov.uk to check the validity of a car's current MoT certificate, plus the history of all of its MoTs, including failure points and advisories. You will need the vehicle's registration mark and the MoT test number from the certificate to do this.

Date of test:		03/12/2008
Certificate issue refused (Fail)		
Odometer reading:		71,494 Miles
Test number:		1528784383
Test station name:		M J MOTORS BIRSTALL LTD
Test station number:		
Test station telephone number:		
Test class:		IV
Reason(s) for refusal to issue Certificate		
Nearside Windscreen wiper does not clear the windscreen effectively (8.2.2)		
Offside Headlamp not working on main beam (1.7.5a)		
Both Stop lamp remains on when the brakes are released (1.2.1e)		
Parking brake lever has no reserve travel (3.1.6b)		
Front to rear Brake pipe excessively corroded (3.6.B.2c)		
Offside Front brake disc excessively pitted (3.5.1h)		
Nearside Rear parking brake recording little or no effort (3.7.A.7a)		
Offside Rear parking brake recording little or no effort (3.7.A.7a)		
Nearside Front suspension has excessive play in a upper suspension ball joint (2.5.B.1a)		

motinfo.direct.gov.uk provides a free MoT history for a car, providing you have its registration number and MoT test number, or document reference number.

Where is the car?
If the Seven replica you intend to view and potentially purchase is a few hundred miles away, you may feel there is more reason to buy it there and then, and not waste your time and money with more than one visit. This, however, is a bad idea: look at every potential purchase with a view not to buy it. With this in mind, if a car is some distance away, make sure you have a means of getting home without it.

Where can I find cars for sale?
You can find most types of car for sale online through Autotrader, Car and Classic, eBay, Gumtree and PistonHeads, but also look at club websites and specialist magazines such as *Kit Car*, *Total Kit Car* and *Complete Kit Car*. If you are looking for a crash-damaged Seven replica to repair and return to roadworthy condition, there are a number of salvage dealers and online auction sites, including Co-Part.

Total Kit Car magazine has its own online classifieds page.

Dealer or private sale?
Some Seven replicas are sold through specialist dealers, including Total Head Turners, Tiger Racing, Sovereign Car Sales, and Robert Sinclair. A dealer may have more limited knowledge of a car's history and how it was built, but may offer a warranty/

guarantee (ask for a printed copy), and finance. Many have a thorough knowledge of Seven replicas, and can ensure a car is in good condition.

A private sale should have the benefit of the owner having more knowledge about the car's history, how it was built, and what problems have been fixed.

Cost of collection and delivery?

A dealer may be used to quoting for delivery by car transporter. A private owner may agree to meet you halfway, but only agree to this after you have seen the car at the vendor's address to validate the documents. If you are buying a crash damaged car, the salvage dealer will probably have their own delivery service.

Viewing time

Always view at the seller's home or business premises. In the case of a private sale, the car's documentation should tally with the seller's name and address. Always arrange to view in daylight, and avoid a wet day. Most cars look better in poor light, or when wet.

Reason for sale?

Do make it one of the first questions. Why is the car being sold, and, more importantly, how long has it been with the current owner? How many previous owners are there? If there are many, why is that? It's not uncommon with older Seven replicas to find a car has been used for a few years, then abandoned in a garage for some time before its next use.

Honesty pays

Ask for an honest opinion on the car and what problems the owner/dealer knows about it. Make it clear you want to know what you need to do to look after the car once you've bought it.

Insurance

Check with your existing insurer before setting out, as your current policy might not cover you to test drive the car, and if you do purchase it, drive it home. There are several insurance policies that cover you for 1-28 days, allowing you to inspect, test drive and collect a car. Websites include dayinsure.com and insuredaily.co.uk.

Motoring bodies including the RAC also provide short-term insurance policies. Specialist insurers including Adrian Flux, Footman James, Blackford Bloor & Co, MSM, and Graham Sykes, all deal with kit car cover. Full contact details can be found in chapter 16.

Bidding on eBay

eBay, and other auction sites, usually have Seven replicas for sale, many of which look tempting, especially when the current bid price is low. However, any cars you intend to bid on should be inspected first to make sure you know what you may be buying. Even an abandoned project or crash damaged, but repairable model, should be looked at to make sure you know what you are letting yourself in for. It's also essential to inspect the car and see the supporting documentation to make sure it actually exists, is correctly registered and legal.

When bidding, set yourself a maximum price and stick to it. Look out for automatic bids that will appear a few seconds after you have made your own bid. You may want to use them yourself to help maintain a maximum value you are willing to pay.

Buying at auction

If the intention is to buy at auction, see chapter 10 for further advice.

Payment methods

Most sellers prefer to deal in cash, unless you are willing to pay by cheque or an inter-bank transfer and wait for the funds to become available. A bankers draft is, in theory, as good as cash, but the increase in fakes means you can only accept this type of payment if your bank can verify it immediately.

Cash is often a tempting and effective method of haggling, as the seller knows the sale can be completed quickly.

Professional examination

If you want a second opinion on a potential purchase, there's no harm in paying a mechanic or motoring body such as the AA or RAC to professionally inspect a car. Expect to pay ⬤80-100 for a written report, but don't expect such bodies to have an in depth knowledge of the kit car industry or Lotus Seven replicas. In the UK a cheaper and simpler inspection is an MoT test to ensure the vehicle is roadworthy. Some kit car manufacturers, including Tiger Racing, can offer both, including an MoT inspection and an overall assessment of a potential purchase.

An MoT helps to determine whether a potential purchase is roadworthy.

Check with the manufacturer

If you are looking to buy a Caterham 7, Westfield, Tiger or a similar model that has a good reputation, and consequently a higher price than other Seven replicas, consult the manufacturer to see whether they have any records for the car in question. Some Seven replicas can be built to resemble a genuine Caterham 7 with the correct badging, but they are not worth as much. If a car is being sold as a Caterham 7, make sure you know how to check that it is a genuine Caterham.

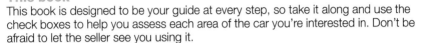

6 Inspection equipment
– these items will really help

This book
This book is designed to be your guide at every step, so take it along and use the check boxes to help you assess each area of the car you're interested in. Don't be afraid to let the seller see you using it.

Reading glasses (if you need them for close work)
You may need reading glasses to read documents and make close up inspections.

Torch
A torch with fresh batteries will be useful for peering into the wheelarches and under the car.

Probe
A small screwdriver can be used – with care – as a probe, particularly along any dirt covered chassis rails. With this you should be able to check any areas of severe corrosion, but be careful – if it's really bad the screwdriver might go right through the metal!

A torch can help to inspect brake lines, and look for leaks under the car.

Overalls and gloves
Be prepared to get dirty. Take along a pair of overalls, if you have them, and a few pairs of disposable gloves.

Mirror on a stick
Fixing a mirror at an angle on the end of a stick may seem odd, but you'll probably need it to check the condition of the underside of the car. It will also help you to peer into some of the important crevices. You can use it, together with the torch, along the underside of the chassis and floor. You're looking for accident damage, signs of where the car has bottomed out, and corrosion.

Digital camera
If you have a digital camera, take it along so that you can later study some areas of the car closely. You can even hold it under the car to take pictures of areas you cannot see. Take a picture of any part of the car that causes you concern, and seek a friend or specialist's opinion.

A digital camera or a camera phone is useful for noting problems you find, and asking others for a second opinion.

A friend, preferably a knowledgeable enthusiast
Ideally, have a friend or knowledgeable enthusiast accompany you: a second opinion is always valuable. If nobody is available, find out if you can call someone when inspecting the car who can offer advice.

Trolley jack, axle stands or ramps
Checking underneath a car is essential to make sure there are no loose fittings or accident damage. It also helps to raise the wheels and check wheel bearings and suspension components. However, find out if the seller is willing to let you do this, and whether you have to bring along your own equipment. If you decide to use a trolley jack to raise the car, secure it with at least one axle stand.

Using a trolley jack (ALWAYS with axle stands or ramps too) helps you to examine the underside of a car, but check that the owner is happy for you to do this.

Paperwork

HPI and MoT checks have been outlined in chapter five and should be conducted before you inspect a potential purchase. Other countries will have similar official roadworthiness checks and vehicle history checking companies. When you arrive to look at the car, a good starting point is to ignore it initially, and ask for the paperwork relating to it first. Start with the registration certificate, making sure the owner's name and address is the same as the person you are buying the car from. You will be able to see on the front of this certificate the number of former owners and whether it has been recorded with accident damage (this should have been

This Locost, built by Andy Thomas, has a chassis number displayed on a plaque attached to the bulkhead, and a number stamped into the chassis. Both should be checked.

detected with the HPI check). Look inside the registration certificate for the Vehicle Identification Number (VIN) and make sure this is the same on the car. The VIN is usually stamped into the chassis in the engine bay area, and also displayed on a separate plate. Ask to see other supporting documentation, especially if the car claims to be a particular model, such as a Caterham 7. This is important in ensuring such a car isn't a cheaper recreation.

Spec checks

Don't take the seller's word for it, check the specification of the car, making sure it is a live axle or IRS, that it has alloy uprights or Hi-Spec brakes, etc, as advertised. Check the engine is the correct type, and what category of emissions it falls into (essential for the MoT in the UK and similar road-worthiness tests in other countries).

Check the specification of the car to make sure it matches what the seller has told you.

Even check that both front tyres and both rear tyres are the same dimensions (the tyres must be the same dimensions across an axle). If you are buying a well sought after car, such as a Caterham 7 R500, find out what parts should be fitted, and make sure they are present.

Initial exterior checks
Look down both sides of the car for rippled panels and differences in paintwork which could indicate resprays and accident damage. Look at the paintwork from different angles to help spot scratches, different shades of paint, and damage. GRP panels including the nose cone, wings, bonnet and rear tub may have spider cracks or faded paintwork. Aluminium panels and wheels can oxidise and turn opaque.

Sit in the driver's seat
Sit in the driver's seat to see if you can operate the foot pedals without stamping on the brake and accelerator at the same time. If your feet don't fit in the footwell, or are too large for the pedals, there's little point in progressing any further, as you cannot safely drive this car without making some modifications. Similarly, if you have to squeeze into the driver's seat, then you must think hard about whether you really want this car.

Check the steering wheel and column are secure, and that all the required switches for lights and indicators are present, along with essential instruments.

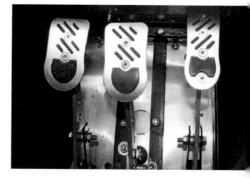

Some pedals can be adjusted to create more space between them. Make sure you can operate them all individually.

These armchair-sized seats are comfortable, but take up a lot of room.

Hidden damage

Look underneath the car, inside the engine bay, and around the suspension points for signs of accident damage. Such damage can be as seemingly superficial as a dent in a chassis rail, but it could indicate more problems and expensive repairs.

Build quality

Look underneath for neat rows of blind rivets attaching the floor to the chassis, and evenly spaced P-clips securing brake pipes and fuel lines (if visible). Check that locking nuts have been fitted to suspension components and that stainless steel fixings are used throughout. Such detail suggests the car has been built with attention to detail, not simply bolted together as fast as possible. Check panel gaps are consistent and components such as lights are evenly spaced. If the finish of such aspects of the build is poor, this may be reflected in the price, but it also presents you with the problem of rectifying them.

Engine bay

There are few plausible excuses for not having a neat engine installation with most of the wiring concealed and clutter hidden away. Seven replica engine bays are spacious enough to allow all of the required components to be fitted without cramming them together. Look for tired wiring that may need renewing, corrosion of chassis rails, engine mounts and exhaust fittings, and try to rock the engine to make sure it is securely mounted.

This dent in the rear chassis rail can affect the suspension geometry and tracking of the road wheels.

The build of a Seven replica can be meticulous, or thrown together, and this is reflected in the overall finish.

There's room inside a Seven replica's engine bay to neatly fit all the required components.

Front wing stays can corrode and break. They're straightforward to weld together again, but check they are sufficiently solid.

The engine's cooling system should feature a header tank – fitted higher than the radiator and engine – to ensure efficient cooling.

The weakest point on the exhaust system? These silencers are substantial, so check the mounts.

Don't assume the engine mounts are good. Try to rock the engine to check they are secure.

Ask the seller to move the steering wheel whilst you check the steering linkage and rack for excessive play. Make sure nothing fouls the steering column.

Wiring in the engine bay should be protected with shielding, and adequately fixed to the chassis rails.

Check the bodywork can be replaced if need be. This Westfield has an all-in-one rear body tub with side panels, which can be awkward to renew.

Clam and cycle wings can get battered, so check them carefully for spider cracks.

Outboard front suspension can become corroded.

Inspect the front nose cone and the rear body tub for signs of damage caused by driving into – or being hit by – something.

Inboard rocker arm suspension means the coilovers are hidden away, but still check the dampers for leaks, and the springs for fractures.

Operate all of the switches and make sure the instruments are working. Dodgy or careless wiring can result in malfunctions.

The Toyota 4AGE is reliable, but check the sump isn't rusty and leaking and that oil isn't leaking from external pipes or from the camshaft cover.

Early MX5 engines suffered from noisy tappets – often caused by frequent short journeys.

Rover K-series engines suffer from head gasket trouble, but this is usually cured with an uprated multi-layered gasket and oil rail, plus stronger head bolts and steel locating dowels.

Pinto engines are robust, but can suffer from oil starvation to the cam, often due to a blocked spray pipe.

9 Serious evaluation

– 60 minutes for years of enjoyment

Score each section using the boxes as follows: 4 = excellent; 3 = good; 2 = average; 1 = poor. The totting up procedure is detailed at the end of the chapter. Be realistic in your marking!

The points outlined in chapters seven and eight now need to be further explored, plus there are additional areas of a Seven or replica that need to be inspected. This chapter covers an in-depth inspection, outlining where to look, what to look for, and how any problems you find should be fixed, plus any approximate costs involved.

Safe inspection
Don't take any risks when inspecting a car you may want to purchase. If you want to raise the car and look underneath it, ensure it is adequately and safely supported. For example, as well as a trolley jack, make sure you use axle stands for additional support. Similarly, when looking underneath a vehicle, make sure the wheels are chocked to prevent the car moving, even if the handbrake is on and first gear is selected.

A trolley jack is useful for raising the car and inspecting the suspension and underside, but ALWAYS supplement it with axle stands or ramps.

Corrosion

Rusty kit cars are rare, but the quantity of steel used in the chassis and suspension components means that corrosion is a possibility. Whilst surface corrosion on a chassis can usually be scrubbed off with a wire brush and painted over, if the metalwork has started to crumble away, the entire area will need to be renewed. Such a repair can be more time-consuming than expected, especially if body panels need to be removed.

Light surface corrosion isn't usually a problem, but excessive rust can mean suspension components are stiff, seized or weakened.

The front wishbones are exposed to the elements, so expect some surface corrosion. The ball joints that secure the wishbones to the uprights can be renewed, and are usually commonly found parts (eg Ford Transit drag link at the top, and Austin Maxi ball joint at the bottom). If the bolts that secure the wishbones to the chassis are heavily corroded, they could be seized inside their respective bushes.

Bodywork
The bodywork on most Seven replicas usually consists of a mixture of GRP and

aluminium panels. Closely inspect the bodywork. Damaged or faded paintwork may be revived (temporarily) with a polish or cutting compound, but ultimately, a respray will be required.

GRP can fracture if it undergoes an impact. Look for spider cracks on the arches where stones may have become trapped between the wheel and underside. Similarly, look at the front of the nose cone and the rear of the body for cracks caused by bumps with other cars, or the car in question driving into something.

Bare aluminium looks very effective on a Seven, but eventually it will oxidise and start to look discoloured and non-

Check the gap around the rear wheels is the same on both sides. Any unevenness suggests either accident damage or a poorly-fitted rear tub or wheelarches.

reflective. It can often be revived with a thorough polish and lacquer to help preserve it, but in many cases the better solution is to remove it and fit a new panel. This can be more complicated than it looks, especially on side panels where the front suspension components may need to be dismantled and other bodywork removed.

Make sure all the bodywork is securely fitted, especially the front cycle wings or clam shells. Cycle wings are usually supported with metal stays that are attached to the front uprights. These can be flimsy on some Seven replicas and will eventually break, so make sure they are solid and free from corrosion.

Check the panel fit is even, not only between the bonnet and side panels, but between the wheels and arches. If the gaps between the arches and rear wheels are uneven, the car could have been involved in an accident, or the rear tub or arches haven't been fitted properly.

Road legal

Double-check that the car you intend to buy is road legal. There are various levels of unroadworthiness, all of which should be reflected in the price. If the car is not taxed,

but has an MoT (applicable to the UK) or similar certificate of roadworthiness in other countries, then the cost of the road tax (road fund licence) needs to be taken into account. However, if the car isn't taxed or MoT'd, find out when it was last MoT'd and driven on the road. It may have been several years since the car was driven (read chapter 15 for further details on this subject).

The most troublesome category of a car not being road legal is when it hasn't been officially registered. In the UK, kit-cars/self builds must pass an Individual Vehicle Assessment (IVA) before they can be used on the road. This test costs

In the UK, a kit car such as a Lotus Seven replica must undergo an IVA before it can be registered for use on the road.

approximately ●500, and can be conducted at a number of VOSA test centres in the UK. Other countries will have their own rules and regulations concerning registration of home-built cars, but many have a similar process. If a Seven replica you are looking to purchase has not passed the appropriate road worthiness test for official registration, the cost of the test must be reflected in the price. If such a car hasn't passed the IVA or equivalent, but the seller insists it isn't required, or that the car can be classed in the owner documents as, say, a Mazda special, do not purchase the car.

Paintwork
Bodywork such as the bonnet (hood), nose cone, and side panels are usually constructed from GRP or aluminium. If they are not painted, the GRP will have a coloured gel coat finish instead. The typical paint problems to look for are covered in-depth in chapter 14. Look for deep scratches that cannot be buffed out, and faded paintwork that hasn't been resolved by a thorough polish. Inspect the paintwork in daylight with the car outside, if possible. If the seller claims the bodywork merely needs a professional polish to remove scratches and fading, question why this hasn't been done, and whether it will actually remove all of the imperfections. If a respray is required, make sure this is reflected in the price, and the cost relevant to the standard you want.

Finally, if a car is dirty, ask for it to be washed, or better still, wash it yourself – this is a useful method of inspecting the car's paintwork.

A car for sale should have been washed to allow you to inspect the paintwork.

Engine
Ideally, the engine should be cold when you begin inspecting the car, because a cold start can reveal problems, if they exist. Ask the owner to start the engine whilst you watch the tailpipe of the exhaust. If blue smoke is emitted from the exhaust, this can suggest engine wear. Clouds of oily smoke often indicate hardened valve stem oil seals, a symptom typical of many engines that haven't been used for long

periods of time. If this is the case, further smoke will probably bellow out of the exhaust on overrun (driving down a hill in gear where the engine isn't providing the power to move the car).

When the engine starts, make sure the oil pressure light on the dashboard goes out, and if an oil pressure gauge is fitted, check there is sufficient pressure. As the engine idles, watch the coolant temperature gauge and ask how quickly the engine warms up, and whether a

Check the engine for oil leaks: especially around the rocker cover and sump.

thermostat has been fitted. When the engine has warmed up, raise the revs and watch for oily smoke from the exhaust, which can indicate the piston rings have worn. White, cloudy smoke from an engine at running temperature often suggests head gasket failure, and this can be further identified when the engine has been switched off and allowed to cool – check the coolant header tank for oil, and inside the oil filler cap for a 'mayonnaise' mixture, which suggests oil and coolant are mixing because the head gasket has failed.

Finally, look all around the engine for signs of oil leaks, especially around the sump, rocker cover, and where it mates to the gearbox (rear main oil seal).

Gearbox

In most cases, a Seven replica will have a Ford Type 9 or MT75 gearbox if it has a car engine, or a sequential gearbox if it has a motorbike engine. Ford gearboxes will usually have the gear stick mounted on the propshaft tunnel. Check there is sufficient space to select all gears without fouling the dashboard. Make sure you can select reverse and all the forward gears – the Type 9 and MT75 have five forward gears, whereas earlier Ford Rocket boxes, for instance, have four. Check there is around two thirds of upward travel on the clutch pedal before the clutch reaches biting point. Ask how the clutch is operated, whether cable or hydraulic.

Check the operation of all gears on a manual gearbox, and make sure the gear stick doesn't foul the dashboard.

Motorbike gearboxes are sequential, and can be operated mechanically using a paddle shift.

Motorbike engines and gearboxes are slightly more complicated, and if you haven't driven one before, don't be ashamed to admit this. Find out exactly how to change up and down the gears. In most cases, a mechanical paddle shift or stick is used, although more expensive setups use electric solenoids, with buttons on the steering wheel to make gear changes. Make sure you can confidently change up and down the gears, and find out how to maintain the gearchange mechanism.

One of the most important aspects of motorbike-engined Seven replicas concerns travelling backwards. There is no reverse gear on a motorbike's gearbox, so an electric reverse is often fitted to Seven replicas. If such a device is fitted, find out how to operate it. If nothing is fitted, think carefully about whether you need a reverse, and, if so, make sure this is reflected in the price. Most reverse kits cost around ●350.

Front suspension

The majority of Lotus Seven replicas feature upper and lower wishbones at the front, with inboard or outboard coilovers. Outboard coilovers are usually mounted between the lower wishbone and chassis, whereas inboard coilovers operate via a rocker arm assembly.

Whatever the suspension design, it will usually feature upper and lower ball joints to connect the wishbones to the upright. Find out what make of ball joints are used – popular types include a Ford Transit drag link for the upper ball joint, and an Austin Maxi for the lower. Worn ball joints can be tested by raising and supporting a front corner of the car and waggling the road wheel. This can also help to detect a worn wheel bearing and track rod end.

Check there are no leaks around the damper, and that the coil spring isn't fractured. If the damper is adjustable, make sure the adjuster isn't seized: it's usually a small knob on the side of the damper.

Inspect the wishbone bushes for signs of damage and perishing. Look at their respective mountings on the chassis for signs of corrosion and damage.

A common front suspension setup found on many Seven replicas: featuring upper and lower double wishbones secured with a Ford Transit drag link at the top, and an Austin Maxi or Metro/MGF ball joint at the bottom.

Rear suspension

The rear suspension setup on Lotus Seven replicas varies depending on whether there's a live axle at the rear (a large solid axle with no visible driveshafts), or an independent rear suspension (IRS) setup, with a small differential mounted in the middle of the chassis and driveshafts connecting it to the hubs. Live axles often have coilovers near each rear wheel, and connecting arms between the axle and chassis to hold it in position. Some early Dutton

An independent rear suspension (IRS) setup can consist of upper and lower wishbones with a coilover, as displayed on this Striker.

Phaetons had leaf springs. A Panhard rod is often fitted to help reduce sideways movement of the live axle.

Some IRS setups consist of conventional upper and lower wishbones with coilovers. Other variations include a De Dion tube, or the entire rear suspension setup from the Ford Sierra. Whatever the suspension setup, make sure the mounting points on the chassis are solid and free from corrosion, bushes are not perished, coil springs are not broken and dampers are not leaking.

Brakes

The braking system from the Ford Sierra is one of the most popular setups on Seven replicas, which features single piston callipers at the front, with vented discs, and either drums at the rear, or single piston callipers and solid discs incorporating a mechanical handbrake mechanism. This can be modified with lighter, aftermarket alloy callipers, featuring drilled and grooved discs and performance brake pads. Other donor vehicle braking systems are taken from the Ford Escort Mk2, Cortina, Capri, Mazda MX-5 (Miata), and the Vauxhall Chevette. In some cases, these are a favoured upgrade over the Sierra because they offer lighter components, including uprights and callipers. Find out what type of brakes have been fitted and inspect their condition; look for perished flexi-hoses, corroded pipework and pitted or worn discs.

Most Seven replicas should have a dual circuit braking system where there are either two pipes leading from one brake master cylinder to provide braking to the front and rear, or separate master cylinders for the front and rear brakes. Very few are servo assisted, but depending on the choice of brake master cylinder(s) and other components, the brakes may feel wooden and ineffective. If the brake pedal needs to travel 25-50mm/1-2in before the brakes feel as though they are biting, the choice of bore size in the master cylinder may be wrong – providing there's no air in the hydraulic system. If the brakes feel wooden and

Ford Sierra hubs, uprights, and brakes are a popular setup on many Seven replicas. They're not the lightest, but are cheap and readily available.

ineffective, the wrong pads may have been fitted, those which require heat before they start to bite. During a test drive, brake at high and low speeds and think about how confident you feel about stopping in an emergency, or braking hard before a corner on a trackday. If the brakes make you feel nervous, ask the seller how they can be improved and whether there are any known problems.

Check the handbrake works and find out what components are fitted. Rear drum brakes usually use standard components, whereas rear disc brakes are sometimes an aftermarket item from Rally Design or other specialists, and are based on the VW Golf.

Steering

The steering rack from the Ford Escort Mk2 is one of the most common components found on the majority of Lotus Seven replicas. It is so popular that specialists such as Rally Design stock them as brand new items with quick rack conversions. The steering column can often be from the Ford Sierra, Escort, Fiesta, Mazda MX-5, or similar cars. Make sure the steering column is securely fitted, with no movement or play when you pull it up and down, and rock it from side to side. Remove the bonnet and check the column and rack doesn't foul anything when the steering wheel is turned and that there's no play in the universal

The Ford Escort Mk2 steering rack is a popular choice. Make sure it is securely clamped to the chassis.

joints. Similarly, check the road wheels don't foul the bodywork and the brake flexible hoses aren't over-stretched on full lock. Try to see how the steering column has been mounted to the chassis. It should be fitted with clamps or bolts, and must be very securely mounted to avoid movement that can affect the car's handling.

Electrics, dashboard and instruments

Make sure the battery is securely fitted; most reside in the engine bay, next to the bulkhead. Trace the wiring to the fuse box and relays, and check they are all easily identifiable. If the seller has a wiring diagram or other details, this will be useful to help trace any electrical faults in the future.

Inspect all visible wiring, ensuring it is securely located with P-clips, plastic trunking, or zip ties, and doesn't foul any

Wiring should be tidy, organised and secure.

moving or hot components. Finally, test all electrical components, ranging from the horn and indicators, to the headlights and foglight. With the engine running, operate as many components as possible to make sure the alternator and battery can cope and that any fuses don't blow. Whilst doing this, check all the dashboard instruments work properly.

Wheels and tyres

Inspect the wheels for signs of damage. If locking nuts/bolts are fitted, make sure the key to undo them is present and fits. Examine the tread on the tyres for signs of uneven wear, which usually suggests the tracking needs adjusting, or the camber is excessive. Lotus Seven replicas are light, so tyre wear is unusual. Most tyres have a lifespan – six years maximum is recommended – after which they should be renewed, especially if you intend to drive the car at high speed on trackdays or in competitive racing, so find out the age of the tyres.

The tyre may be in good condition, but this one has a code on the sidewall that indicates it was manufactured in 2002. Consequently, it is well past its use-by date.

Interior trim

The level of interior trim in Lotus Seven replicas ranges between basic no-frills to luxurious. Whatever the condition, make sure the seats and seatbelts are securely fitted. If carpets and trim panels are fitted, they must be secure, but capable of being removed should

The interior may look clean and tidy, but make sure the carpets can be removed if they need to be dried, and look for signs of water from the road finding its way in from underneath.

they need to be dried out. Look for signs of water in the footwells – this could indicate gaps in the floor where water from the road could find its way in.

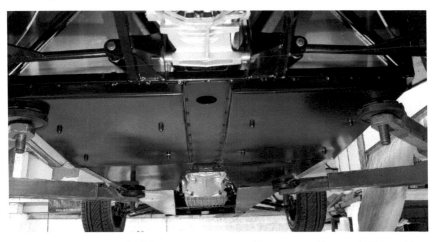

The underneath of this GBS Zero is uncluttered with neat panelling, and all the wiring and pipework is protected from road dirt.

Underbody

Spend a few minutes looking underneath the car; lie on a sheet of cardboard or wear old clothes, and keep a torch with you. Look for the lowest point on the car – usually the sump or rear diff casing – and inspect it for damage and cracks caused by driving over speed bumps, which could result in oil leaks. Check the floor is securely fitted to the chassis and that there are no gaps where water from the road can get in. Look at visible pipework (brake hydralics and fuel feed usually) and make sure it is secured with P-clips or similar fixings.

Weather equipment

Most Lotus Seven replicas don't have any form of weather equipment, but if a windscreen is fitted, it should have wipers, washer jets and some form of a demister. Check this equipment works properly. If doors and a hood are fitted, ask the seller to demonstrate how the hood should be fitted properly. The hood will probably be made from vinyl, with a plastic rear screen, so make sure you can see out of the rear screen and that there are no tears in the hood. Very few hoods are 100% waterproof, so don't ask to throw a bucket of water over it, but make sure it fits on the car and doesn't sag.

Ask to be shown how to put the soft top up and down. Look for tears in the fabric and cracks in the rear screen.

Fuel system

Check the fuel pipes leading from the fuel pump to the fuel filter, fuel regulator (usually fitted with carburettors) and onto the carburettor(s) or injection system; make sure the fuel filter is easy to remove. Operate the accelerator pedal with the engine switched off and check it can fully open the butterfly on the throttle body/bodies or carburettor(s) without fouling anything. Check any throttle linkage (fitted to multiple carburettors) operates freely and can be adjusted if required. If no air filter or gauze is fitted, dirt may be getting sucked into the engine, causing potential damage, so ask why an air filter hasn't been fitted.

Motorcycle engines are often fuelled by carburettors, although later engines use injection systems.

Cooling system

If possible, inspect the condition of the front of the radiator to see if it has been damaged by debris from the road. An electric fan should be fitted to it – check how it is operated (manually or automatically via a thermostat), and if possible, test it. Check all coolant pipes for signs of corrosion, perishing and leaks. When the engine is cold,

The silencer is usually fitted to the side of a Seven replica. Make sure it is secured with a clamp or mount.

look inside the header tank and inspect the condition of the coolant for signs of oil (indicating head gasket failure) and corrosion (lack of anti-freeze).

Exhaust

The exhaust system is usually very straightforward on Lotus Seven replicas, consisting of a manifold that connects to a single pipe with a side-mounted silencer and short exit pipe. Some exhaust systems are routed under the car with exit pipes at the rear, but most are side mounted. With the engine running, listen for leaks around the manifold where it clamps to the engine and at the opposite end. If no catalytic converter is fitted, make sure the engine does not legally require one.

Check the mounting of the exhaust silencer, making sure it is secure, but capable of moving. Most silencers have a rubber mount, which is fixed to the chassis.

Test drive

A Lotus Seven replica should be light and nimble when driven on the road. Depending on the suspension setup (spring rates, damper settings and geometry), and whether lightweight wheels, hubs and uprights have been fitted, the ride quality may either be harsh or fluid-like. Before setting off, make sure you are confident with operating the controls, especially the pedals; practice moving your right foot from the accelerator to the brake pedal. Whilst driving, change up and down gears to check gear changes are trouble free, operate the brakes to ensure they are responsive, and, if possible, drive through the rev range in a low gear to ensure there are no flat spots.

The steering should be light and positive, allowing you to point the car in the desired direction and let it do the work.

Avoid test pilot antics when driving a car you may wish to buy. Take your time, assessing the ride quality, brakes, and steering.

Avoid any heroics when test driving, such as power slides and wheel spins. Whilst you may be concerned with the amount of power such a car has to offer, the point of the test drive is to determine whether it has been properly constructed, so you need to assess whether the car is easy to drive and inspires you with confidence. If the car crashes into potholes, leaves you fighting with the steering wheel on corners, bump-steers over rough surfaces, and skips and hops under acceleration, don't be fooled into thinking this is normal: a correctly set up Seven replica is a fantastic car to drive.

Evaluation procedure
Add up the total points.

Score: 76 = excellent; 57 = good; 38 = average; 19 = poor. Cars scoring over 53 will be completely usable and will require only maintenance and care to preserve condition. Cars scoring between 19 and 39 will require some serious work (at much the same cost regardless of score). Cars scoring between 40 and 52 will require very careful assessment of the necessary repair/restoration costs in order to arrive at a realistic value.

10 Auctions
– sold! Another way to buy your dream

Auction pros & cons
Pros:
Prices will usually be lower than those of dealers or private sellers and you might grab a real bargain on the day. Auctioneers have usually established clear title with the seller. At the venue you can usually examine documentation relating to the vehicle.

Cons:
You have to rely on a sketchy catalogue description of condition and history. The opportunity to inspect is limited and you cannot drive the car. Auction cars are often a little below par and may require some work. It's easy to overbid. There will usually be a buyer's premium to pay in addition to the auction hammer price.

Which auction?
Auctions by established auctioneers are advertised in car magazines and on the auction houses' websites. A catalogue, or a simple printed list of the lots for auction might only be available a day or two ahead, though often lots are listed and pictured on auctioneers' websites much earlier. Contact the auction company to ask if previous auction selling prices are available as this is useful information (details of past sales are often available on websites).

Catalogue, entry fee and payment details
When you purchase the catalogue of the vehicles in the auction, it often acts as a ticket allowing two people to attend the viewing days and the auction. Catalogue details tend to be comparatively brief, but will include information such as 'one owner from new, low mileage, full service history,' etc. It will also usually show a guide price giving you some idea of what to expect to pay, and will tell you what is charged as a 'Buyer's premium.' The catalogue will also contain details of acceptable forms of payment. At the fall of the hammer an immediate deposit is usually required, the balance payable within 24 hours. If the plan is to pay by cash there may be a cash limit. Some auctions will accept payment by debit card. Sometimes credit or charge cards are acceptable, but will often incur an extra charge. A bank draft or bank transfer will have to be arranged in advance with your own bank as well as with the auction house. No car will be released before all payments are cleared. If delays occur in payment transfers then storage costs can accrue.

Buyer's premium
A buyer's premium will be added to the hammer price: don't forget this in your calculations. It is not usual for there to be a further state tax or local tax on the purchase price and/or on the buyer's premium.

Viewing
In some instances it's possible to view on the day, or days before, as well as in the hours prior to the auction. There are auction officials available who are willing

to help out by opening engine and luggage compartments and allowing you to inspect the interior. While the officials may start the engine for you, a test drive is out of the question. Crawling under and around the car as much as you want is permitted, but you can't suggest that the car you are interested in be jacked up, or attempt to do the job yourself. You can ask to see any documentation available.

Bidding

Before you take part in the auction, decide your maximum bid – and stick to it!

It may take a while for the auctioneer to reach the lot you're interested in, so use that time to observe how other bidders behave. When it's the turn of your car, attract the auctioneer's attention and make an early bid. The auctioneer will then look to you for a reaction every time another bid is made, usually the bids will be in fixed increments until the bidding slows, when smaller increments will often be accepted before the hammer falls. If you want to withdraw from the bidding, make sure the auctioneer understands your intentions – a vigorous shake of the head when he or she looks to you for the next bid should do the trick.

Assuming that you're the successful bidder, the auctioneer will note your card or paddle number, and from that moment on you will be responsible for the vehicle.

If the car is unsold, either because it failed to reach the reserve or because there was little interest, it may be possible to negotiate with the owner, via the auctioneers, after the sale is over.

Successful bid

There are two more items to think about; how to get the car home and insurance. If you can't drive the car, your own or a hired trailer is one way, another is to have the vehicle shipped using the facilities of a local company. The auction house will also have details of companies specialising in the transfer of cars.

Insurance for immediate cover can usually be purchased on site, but it may be more cost-effective to make arrangements with your own insurance company in advance, and then call to confirm the full details.

eBay & other online auctions

eBay and other online auctions could land you a car at a bargain price, though you'd be foolhardy to bid without examining the car first, something most sellers encourage. A useful feature of eBay is that the geographical location of the car is shown, so you can narrow your choices to those within a realistic radius of home. Be prepared to be outbid in the last few moments of the auction. Remember, your bid is binding and that it will be very, very difficult to get restitution in the case of a crooked seller fleecing you – caveat emptor!

Be aware that some cars offered for sale in online auctions are 'ghost' cars. Don't part with any cash without being sure that the vehicle actually exists and is as described (usually pre-bidding inspection is possible).

eBay is a useful place to find abandoned Lotus Seven replicas, which are either undergoing repair work and upgrades or haven't been built and registered. Such a project may seem like a bargain, but always try to inspect the car before bidding and make sure you ask all the important questions first, such as if the car has been correctly registered.

Auctioneers
Barons... www.barons-auction.com
Bonhams... www.bonhams.com
British Car Auctions (BCA) www.bca-europe.com or www.british-car-auctions.co.uk
Cheffins .... www.cheffins.co.uk
Christies .... www.christies.com
Coys.. www.coys.co.uk
eBay .... www.ebay.com
H&H .... www.classic-auctions.co.uk
RM .... www.rmauctions.com
Shannons.. www.shannons.com.au
Silver .... www.silverauctions.com

Classic car auctions can often include restoration projects, such as this original
Lotus Seven.

11 Paperwork
– correct documentation is essential!

A home-buil Seven replica will often be accompanied by a large portfolio of photographs, receipts and other documentation, proving it was amateur built (in the UK this is essential for the IVA and registration process). Older examples or factory-built cars won't have such useful information, but in all cases, there are some essential pieces of paper that are required, and this chapter outlines all of them.

Registration documents

All countries/states have some form of registration for private vehicles, whether it's like the American 'pink slip' system, or the British 'log book' system.

It is essential to check that the registration document is genuine, that it relates to the car in question, and that all the vehicle's details are correctly recorded, including chassis/VIN and engine numbers (if these are shown). If you are buying from the previous owner, his or her name and address will be recorded in the document; this will not be the case if you are buying from a dealer.

Carefully check the registration documents for the car, making sure the details are correct.

In the UK the current (Euro-aligned) registration document is named V5C, and relates to the car's specification, the details of the owner, the number of previous owners, and whether the car has been written-off or accident damaged.

In the UK the DVLA will provide details of earlier keepers of the vehicle upon payment of a small fee, and much can be learned in this way.

Roadworthiness certificate

Most country/state administrations require that vehicles are regularly tested to prove they are safe to use on the public highway, and do not produce excessive emissions. In the UK this test (the MoT) is carried out at approved testing stations, for a fee. In the UK the test is required on an annual basis once a vehicle becomes three years old – details of past tests and the validity of a current test can be checked online (see chapter 5).

Of particular relevance for older cars is that the certificate issued includes the mileage reading recorded at the test date and, therefore, becomes an

The new MoT certificate in the UK is easy to forge, so double-check it online at motinfo.direct.gov.uk.

independent record of that car's history. Ask the seller if previous certificates are available. Without an MoT the vehicle should be trailored to its new home, unless you insist that a valid MoT is part of the deal.

Road tax
The administration of every country/state charges some kind of tax for the use of its road system, the actual form of the 'road licence,' and how it is displayed, varying enormously from country to country.

Whatever the form of the 'road licence,' it must relate to the vehicle carrying it and must be present and valid if the car is to be driven on the public highway legally. The value of the license will depend on the length of time it will continue to be valid.

In the UK, a car that is not taxed must be declared SORN (Statutory Off Road Notification), which means it cannot be driven on the road, unless it is going to an MoT testing station. Similarly, if a car is not insured, but has a valid road licence (car tax), this must be cashed in and the vehicle declared

Check the road tax applies to the car you are looking to buy.

as a SORN. Such rules were introduced in 2012 and aim to reduce the problem of uninsured drivers with taxed cars.

Service history
Factory built Caterham 7s and similar cars such as Westfields often appeal to non-DIY enthusiasts, who may use a specialist or local garage for servicing and repairs. Consequently, such cars often have a full service history in the form of receipts or a book. If you are looking for such a car, consult these manufacturers and any recommended dealers who sell these cars to see if any are available.

12 What's it worth?
– let your head rule your heart

The value of a Seven replica is often based on the price of similar models with a similar specification. However, some features don't add value: such as expensive electronic gear shift buttons on a motorcycle-engined car instead of a mechanically operated shifter. The following chapter helps to break down many of the cost implications to help you decide whether a particular Lotus Seven replica is a good buy or not.

Undesirable features
Whilst tatty features of a car (worn seats, scraped wheels, spaghetti wiring) may be

reflected in the price, features that you do not like are often down to taste, so cannot be used to reduce the amount you are willing to pay; but think carefully about how much it will cost to change them. If you don't like the dashboard instruments, budget for around ●300 for a new set of clocks (unless you can take a set from a donor vehicle and make them work). If the brakes feel wooden until they are warm, a new set of softer pads may solve the problem for around ●20-30. Clam shell-style wings can be changed to cycle wings. Similarly, there may be features you don't like because they alter the look or driving characteristics of the car. If the ride

Even if the springs and dampers are too harsh, and affect ride quality, it often won't bring down the car's sale price.

quality is harsh because the suspension springs are too stiff and the wheels are too large, then it may be difficult to haggle, despite, in your opinion, the wrong choice of components having been fitted.

Valueless features
Some features of a Lotus Seven replica may cost more to fit, but don't help to increase the price tag of the car when it's up for sale. The aforementioned gear change system at the start of this chapter is one such example. Simple engine upgrades, such as a stainless steel exhaust system, induction kit, and fast road cams, rarely push up the price tag: they just make the car a little more appealing to potential buyers. A windscreen with hood and side screens

The Zetec engine in this Locost is fuelled by motorbike carbs. It's a desirable feature, but rarely helps to push up the price.

rarely adds value. If anything, such features often work in your favour, and help to narrow-down your choice of cars to inspect.

Desirable points

There are some aspects to a Lotus Seven replica that make it more desirable than others. Irrespective of make, motorcycle engines generally demand a higher price tag over car engines, unless the car engine is extra special (V8, turbo or supercharged with bags of bhp). Factory built cars can sometimes justify a premium price tag, as do those built by specialists or professionals, but the evidence of good workmanship and use of the right fixings (stainless steel nuts and bolts, for instance), needs to be seen. The overall finish of a car can be the key point to its value: whether it's tatty and an absolute bargain, or immaculate, but cheaper than buying a brand new factory car. However, there are lots of exceptions within each model, for example, a tatty Hayabusa-engined Locost will probably sell for more than the same model in concours condition that's only armed with a 100bhp Ford Crossflow under the bonnet.

This Chevrolet V8, installed in a Roadrunner SR2, helps to boost the car's price tag.

Non-registered race cars

There are many race cars and trackday cars that cannot be driven on the road because they have not been submitted for the relevant test and registration process. However, this may not be reflected in the price, because such a car is purely intended for race circuit use. In the case of a race car that has already competed in events, it will have usually passed some form of scrutiny, which involves assessing fire protection, the roll cage, seat, and harness. Trackday cars do not have to comply with any regulations. If you are purchasing such a car and intend to register it for road use, you may find it needs several alterations to pass a test such as the IVA in the UK. If you intend to race or use it for trackdays, it is essential the car is fully checked to make sure it is safe for this purpose.

– it'll take longer and cost more than you think

Roadworthy and ready

Buying a Lotus Seven replica that's registered, taxed, and tested for road use, is the quickest way to acquiring such a car and driving it. You may want to alter a few things to your own taste and modify certain aspects, but otherwise, this is the fastest approach to ownership and driving on the road. It does, however, require a large sum of money straight away, unlike the other options mentioned in this chapter where costs can be spread over months or years.

Kit build

Building a Lotus Seven replica from a kit allows you to choose the specification and determine the level of finish. The overall cost of the car can sometimes be spread across many months, instead of paying for everything at once. The disadvantages of this approach concern time and, in many cases, final costs. Most Lotus Seven replicas take 100-200hrs to build, unless a lot of the work is already done for you. The final cost of a build can often be more expensive than expected, especially if you become more ambitious with the specification.

Abandoned projects

Part-built kit cars are always appearing on eBay and other selling websites. With promises of 'all parts to finish,' '95% complete,' and 'only requires minor wiring,' it's often tempting to dream of spending a few weekends in the garage and emerging with a completed car at a fraction of the cost of a new kit or factory build. However, the reality is often less rosy. An abandoned build may be because the owner lacks the skills to complete the project, so the work that has been done could be very poor. Whilst such a project may seem cheap, be prepared to undo all of the work and start again, potentially saving money, but wasting more of your time.

IVA and registration

Kit cars such as Lotus Seven replicas have to be tested and registered to allow them to be driven on the road, although most countries don't stipulate anything if a car is being only used on trackdays. If you are building a kit or finishing off an abandoned project, find out how much these procedures will cost and what is involved. In the UK, budget for around ●500 for the IVA and registration.

Building your own Lotus Seven replica means you can choose its specification, and ensure that all the parts are correctly fitted.

An abandoned project may require just as much time as building a kit from scratch, especially if you have to fix problems and resolve wiring issues.

An unregistered Seven replica in the UK requires an IVA; a safety check to ensure the car has been properly constructed.

14 Paint problems

– bad complexion, including dimples, pimples and bubbles

The majority of Lotus Seven replicas are clothed in GRP and aluminium panels. These are either painted, left bare in the case of aluminium, or are of GRP with a coloured gel coat. Paint faults generally occur due to lack of protection and/or maintenance, or to poor preparation prior to a respray or touch-up. Some of the following conditions may be present in the car you're looking at.

Swirl marks

Polishing can leave tiny circular scratches in the paintwork, especially if dirt has got in the way. Such damage can often be removed by thoroughly cleaning the area, then using a good quality polish with a dual action random orbital polisher. The damage can be polished out by hand, but will take a lot longer.

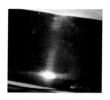

Flatting and poor-quality polishing has resulted in these swirl marks.

Deep scratches

A scratch that has gone through the layers of paint may be difficult to polish out, as most of the paintwork will have to be removed. Such scratches can be touched-up with paint, but if there are several of them, a respray is the best solution.

Orange peel

This appears as an uneven paint surface, similar to the appearance of the skin of an orange. The fault is caused by the failure of atomized paint droplets to flow into each other when they hit a surface. It's sometimes possible to rub out the effect with proprietary paint cutting/rubbing compound or very fine grades of abrasive paper. A respray may be necessary in severe cases. Consult a bodywork repairer/paint shop for advice on the particular car.

These deep scratches will be difficult to remove through polishing. A paint repair will help to hide them, but a respray is a better option.

Cracking

Severe cases are likely to have been caused by too heavy an application of paint, or filler beneath the paint. Also, insufficient stirring of the paint before application can lead to the components being improperly mixed, and cracking can result. Incompatibility with the paint already on the panel can have a similar effect. To rectify the problem it's necessary to rub down to a smooth, sound finish before respraying the problem area. Spider cracks can emerge on flat panels where an object has collided with the panel from underneath, resulting in paint damage to the exterior (looks like a series of cracks in the shape of a spider).

This spider crack has been caused by an object puncturing the panel from underneath. It's common on wheel arches.

Crazing

Sometimes the paint takes on a crazed rather than a cracked appearance when the problems mentioned under 'Cracking' are present. This problem can also be caused by a reaction between the underlying surface and the paint. Paint removal and respraying the problem area is usually the only solution.

Micro blistering

Usually the result of a cheap respray where inadequate heating has allowed moisture to settle on the car before spraying. Consult a paint specialist, but usually damaged paint will have to be removed before partial or full respraying. Can also be caused by car covers that don't breathe.

Fading

Some colours, especially reds, are prone to fading if subjected to strong sunlight for long periods without the benefit of polish protection. Sometimes proprietary paint restorers and/or paint cutting/rubbing compounds will retrieve the situation. Often a respray is the only real solution.

Faded paintwork can sometimes be revived with a thorough polish. A quick polish by hand will last a few weeks.

Peeling

Often a problem with metallic paintwork when the sealing lacquer becomes damaged and begins to peel off. Poorly applied paint may also peel. The remedy is to strip and start again!

Dimples

Dimples in the paintwork are caused by the residue of polish (particularly silicone types) not being removed properly before respraying. Paint removal and repainting is the only solution.

Dents

Small dents are usually easily cured by the 'Dentmaster,' or equivalent process, that sucks or pushes out the dent (as long as the paint surface is still intact). Companies offering dent removal services usually come to your home, but this can only fix dents in aluminium (GRP doesn't dent, it cracks). Severely dented panels are often easier to replace.

The gel coat paintwork on this rear arch has been chipped away by road debris.

Chipped gel coat

If a GRP panel has been drilled through or an edge has been damaged, the resin and fibreglass can become chipped and the damage may need repairing with more resin and a skim of filler.

Paintless remedies

If you're not keen on painting panels, then an alternative solution to fixing poor paintwork is to cover it in vinyl. There are a number of vinyl wrapping specialists, suppliers and DIY kits. Parts such as the front wings, nose cone and bonnet can be removed and wrapped separately.

Vinyl wrapping is an alternative approach to painting, and can look just as good.

15 Problems due to lack of use
– just like their owners, cars need exercise!

Hobby cars like Lotus Seven replicas are rarely used as everyday transport, and can become neglected for months, or even years. This chapter deals with some of the common issues caused as a result of neglect, and how to identify them when looking at a potential purchase.

Seized components

The sliders inside single piston brake callipers can seize, often resulting in ineffective braking (they pull the outer brake pad onto the brake disc), but can be drifted out and lubricated. Brake calliper pistons can corrode and seize: sometimes this can be fixed by removing the brake pads, gently applying the brake, and cleaning the exposed part of the piston, before levering it back inside the calliper.

The handbrake may be stuck if it has been left on. If drum brakes are fitted at the rear, tap the sides with a soft-faced mallet to help release the brake shoes. Rear disc brakes may have a mechanical handbrake calliper which will need releasing.

The clutch's friction plate may become stuck to the flywheel because of corrosion, resulting in no gear selection. This can sometimes be resolved by starting the car in gear with your foot off the clutch pedal.

The alloy road wheels can stick against the hubs, but are usually easy to free with a large block of wood and a hammer.

Corrosion can result in seized nuts and bolts and suspension bushes stuck onto their mounting bolts.

Road salt and rain has corroded these rear suspension components and fixings.

Fluids

Brake fluid absorbs water from the atmosphere and should be renewed every two years. Old fluid with a high water content can cause corrosion and pistons/callipers to seize (freeze), which can cause brake failure when the water turns to vapour near hot braking components.

If the coolant hasn't been renewed, or a specialist lifelong product used, then it can cause corrosion inside the engine (particularly engines with aluminium blocks and/or cylinder heads) and the radiator.

Old, acidic oil can corrode bearings and leave thick deposits inside the sump, which can block the pickup pipe, pump and any spray bars (the latter common on Pinto engines).

The tread may be sufficient, but the cracks in this tyre's sidewall make it dangerous to use; it should be renewed.

Tyre problems

Tyres that have had the weight of the car on them in a single position for some time will develop flat spots, resulting in some (usually temporary) vibration. The tyre walls may also have cracks or blister-like bulges, meaning new tyres are needed.

People tend to forget that two-seater sports cars are often a second car, so they do less mileage than everyday cars. Although tyre wear is not a real factor, the age of the tyres is. Tyres over six years of age are generally considered to be nearing the end of their natural life, regardless of mileage.

Rubber and plastic

Radiator hoses may have perished and split, possibly resulting in the loss of all coolant. Gaitors/boots can crack. Wiper blades will harden. Metalastic mountings can crack and de-bond.

Recent changes to the MoT in the UK mean that if a trackrod end or ball joint boot is cracked, it will now fail. This also applies to rear driveshaft boots.

Suspension dampers

Dampers can leak, resulting in a harsh ride quality. The exposed shaft of a damper can corrode through lack of use. If it's rusty, it can damage the seals inside the damper when it starts to work again.

Electrics

GRP cars often have earthing trouble because the plastic bodywork insulates rather than conducts electricity. Damp will corrode electrical connections. Old wiring becomes brittle and starts to break down. Sparkplug electrodes will often have corroded in an unused engine, and the HT leads may have broken down. If you're having trouble starting the engine, renew these components. The car's battery will be of little use if it hasn't been charged for many months. Look around and underneath the battery for signs of leaking battery acid: if it gets into the chassis it will result in corrosion.

Rotting exhaust system

Exhaust gas contains a high water content, so exhaust systems corrode very quickly from the inside when the car is not used. Similarly, the fixings for the manifold and system (including the mount for the silencer) can corrode and be difficult to undo.

The dirt adhering around the adjuster at the base of this coilover unit suggests the damper has been leaking.

Old wiring becomes brittle and breaks down, resulting in potential electrical problems.

16 The Community
– key people, organisations and companies in the Seven replica world

This chapter lists many of the clubs and specialists that are involved with Lotus Seven replicas. There is an ever growing and changing list of these useful contacts and a search of the Internet can often reveal some of the latest recruits.

Clubs

7 and Roadster Club Belgium
www.7rcb.be

750 Motor Club
www.750mc.co.uk

Birkin Owners Group
http://autos.groups.yahoo.com/group/
birkinowners

Caterham 7 Club
www.lotussevenclub.com

Clubbies SA (Australia)
www.clubbiessa.com

Dax Sporting Club
www.daxsportingclub.com

Donkervoort Touring Club (Netherlands)
www.donkervoorttouringclub.nl

Dutton Owners Club
www.duttonownersclub.co.uk

Elfin Owners and Drivers Club (Australia)
www.elfinheritage.com.au

GKD Owners Club
www.gkdoc.com

JKPSC (Sylva/Raw Striker)
www.jpsc.org.uk

Locost Builders Forum
www.locostbuilders.co.uk

Locust Enthusiasts Club
www.locust.org.uk

The Robin Hood Owners' Club can be seen at all the major kit car shows in the UK. www.rhocar.org

Mac#1 Motorsports Owners Club
www.m1moc.com

MK Owners Club
www.mkownersclub.net

Nise7ens
www.nise7ens.net

Quantum Owners Club
www.quantumowners.co.uk

Seven IG Germany
www.seven-ig.de

Super Seven Club Netherlands
www.sevenclub.nl

Tiger Owners Club
www.tigerownersclub.co.uk

Westfield Sports Car Club
www.wscc.co.uk

Annual kit car shows in the UK
The Kent Kit Car Show (Detling)
When: mid-April

Kit car shows allow you to speak to numerous manufacturers and owners.

01406 372600
www.detlingkitcarshow.co.uk

National Kit Car Motor Show
(Stoneleigh)
When: first May Bank holiday
01406 372600
www.nationalkitcarmotorshow.co.uk
www.nationalkitcarshow.co.uk

National Kit Car Festival (Newark)
When: mid-June
01526 320721
www.kitcarshow.co.uk

Donington Kit Car Show
When: early September
01903 236268
www.doningtonkitcarshow.com

Exeter Kit Car Motor Show
When: end of October
01406 372600
www.exeterkitcarshow.co.uk

Manufacturers – UK
Caterham Cars

01883 333700
www.caterham.co.uk

DJ Sports Cars International (Dax)
01279 442661
www.daxcars.co.uk

Fenspeed Motorsport
01733 319193
www.fenspeed-motorsport.com

GKD Sports Cars
08709 104108
www.gkdsportscars.com

Great British Sports Cars
01623 860990
www.greatbritishsportscars.co.uk

Mac#1 Motorsports
0114 2511016
www.mac1motorsports.co.uk

MK Sports Cars
01709 816 138
www.mksportscars.com

MNR
01423 780299
www.mnrltd.co.uk

Quantum Sports Cars
01548 550660
www.quantumcars.eu

Raw Striker
01432 371169
www.striker-cars.co.uk

Roadrunner Racing
07802 766128
www.roadrunnerracing.net

Southways Sports Cars
01329 220755
www.southwaysautomotive.co.uk/SSC2

Tiger Racing
01945 461423
www.tigerracing.com

Vindicator Cars
07703 289833
www.vindicator.co.uk

Westfield Sports Cars
01384 400077
www.westfield-sportscars.co.uk

Manufacturers – Europe
Donkervoort (Netherlands)
0320 267 050
www.donkervoort.com

Faroux Sports Cars (Netherlands)
www.farouxsportscars.com

Luso Motors (Portugal)
http://lusomotors.com

Race Tech (Estonia)
www.racetech.ee

RCB (Germany)
08076 8500
www.rcb7.de

Great British Sports Cars produces the
Zero, but it also caters for older Robin
Hood models.

MNR's workshop is often full of cars,
including its own take on the Lotus
Seven, the Vortx.

Tiger Racing not only specialises in kit
cars, it also restores classics – including
original Lotus Sevens – and maintains
modern sports cars.

Sniper Factory (Belgium)
+32-89-56 45 71
www.sniperfactory.cc

Manufacturers – rest of world
Almac (New Zealand)
04 528 8680
www.almac.co.nz

Arrow Sports Cars (Australia)
03 9551 9083
www.arrowsportscars.com.au

Birkin (South Africa)
www.birkindirect.com

Dala 7 (Sweden)
070 6759220
www.dala7.se

Elfin Sports Cars (Australia)
03 9265 9700
www.elfin.com.au

Fraser Cars (New Zealand)
09 482 0071
www.fraser.co.nz

Kevant Motors (Australia)
02 439 63528

McGregor Motorsport (New Zealand)
03 388 3838
http://mcgregormotorsport.co.nz

Nota Sports and Racing Cars (Australia)
02 9651 2529
www.notasportscars.com

PRB (Australia)
www.prbaustralia.com.au

Puma Clubman (Australia)
www.pumaclubman.com

Insurance specialists
A-Plan Insurance
01635 874646

Adrian Flux
0800 081 8989
www.adrianflux.co.uk

Blackford Bloor & Co
0151 356 8776
www.insurance4kitcars.co.uk

Footman James
0843 357 1794
www.footmanjames.co.uk

Gott & Wyne
01492 870991
www.gottandwyne.co.uk

Graham Sykes
01395 255100
www.graham-sykes.co.uk

MSM Insurance
01279 870535
www.msminsurance.co.uk

Osborne and Sons
0871 222 7894
www.kitcarinsurance.co.uk

Performance Direct
0844 573 3549
www.performancedirect.co.uk

The Kit Car and Replica Insurance
0845 373 4777
www.heritage-quote.co.uk

17 Vital statistics
– essential data at your fingertips

Magazines and books

Kit Car magazine (monthly)
www.kit-cars.com

Complete Kit Car (monthly)
www.completekitcar.co.uk

Total Kit Car (bi-monthly)
www.totalkitcar.com

Kit Car (USA) – online
www.kitcar.com

A-Z of Kit Cars
Author: Steve Hole
ISBN: 1844256774

Build your own sports car
Author: Chris Gibbs
ISBN: 1844253910

*Caterham Sevens: The Official Story
of a Unique British Sportscar from
Conception to CSR*
Author: Chris Rees
ISBN: 189987061X

*How to build Tiger Avon or GTA sports
cars for road or track*
Author: Jim Dudley
ISBN: 9781845844332

*How to Build & Modify Sportscar &
Kitcar Suspension & Brakes for Road
& Track – Revised & Updated 3rd Edition*
Author: Des Hammill
ISBN: 9781845842079

UK magazines including *Kit Car* (seen here), *Total Kit Car,* and *Complete Kit Car,* all
provide features and test drive reports on Lotus Seven replicas.

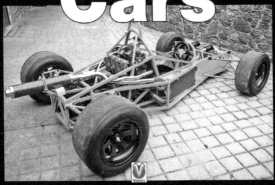

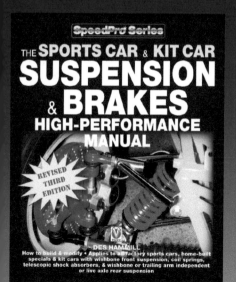

Index